FARMERS ALMANAC! WHAT IS AN ALMANAC AND HOW DO FARMERS USE IT?

(FARMING FOR KIDS)

CHILDREN'S BOOKS ON FARM LIFE

Left Brain Kids

Educational Books for Children

Have you ever wondered how farmers know the coming weather so theyknow when theycan plant and harvest?

What is an almanac? What information can be found in an almanac?

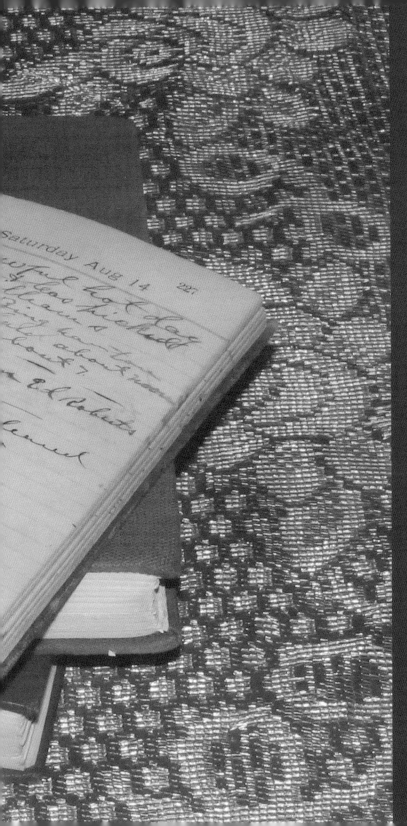

An almanac is an annual or yearly reference book. It gives us information about weather forecasts, farmers' planting dates, tide tables, and crop information arranged according to the calendar of a given year.

Farmers use
almanacs
to know the
best dates for
planting crops.

The almanac is a yearly calendar of statistical information about the phases of the moon, times of sunrise and sunset, tides and many otherthings, along with miscellaneous information and interesting stories.

It outlines each
day of the year
and what it is
likely to hold.

14

15

22

30

21

29

28

ПЯТНИЦ
FRI

ЧЕТВЕРГ
THURSDAY

СРЕДА
WEDNESDAY

ВТОРНИК
TUESDAY

XI

XII

X

The calendar that
you use at home
is actually a
simple almanac!

Two of the most popular almanacs are the Farmers' Almanac(began in 1818) and the Old Farmer's Almanac (1792). Both almanacs are known to be 80% accuratewith their weather predictions.

Both almanacs are known to be 80% accurate with their weather predictions.

The Old Farmer's Almanac is the oldest almanac in North America. It has been published yearly since 1792.

Farmers quickly appreciated The Old Farmer's Almanac. They use it to keep informed of the weather predictions for the upcoming year.

The Old Farmer's Almanac has a hole in the corner. You might be curious what it is for. This is so you can hang the book from a string or a nail.

The Farmers' Almanac gives weather predictions that are based on a secret mathematical and astronomical formula. The formula is said to consider sunspot activity, tidal action, moon phases, planetary positioning and many more factors.

The Farmers' Almanac became popular because of its weather forecasts. Farmers use it when they plan for their annual planting, growing and harvesting efforts.

When farmers plan their crops, they usually turn to one of these almanacs for help.

Farmers or gardeners often wonder when to put in their garden or when to plant their crops.

When seasons change, we experience prolonged summer days and drought. Farmers like to know when the rain will return.

Curious farmers often use an almanac to know when the spring rains will come so they can transplant their seedlings. Farmers use an almanac to know if the season will help the freshly planted seeds to sprout and grow.

In our modern world, many serious farmers still rely on long-range temperature and precipitation charts presented by almanacs. Many people are still influenced by the wealth of information presented in an almanac. Farmers really appreciate the weather predictions given by these books.

As yearly publications, almanacs give us all sorts of information. You may grab one and read it when you're at the library. To make it easier for you, just search for an almanac online and find out what it can offer.

Made in the USA
Lexington, KY
19 October 2016